The Story of Amy Johnson...

Little Wings

F.J. Beerling

Illustrated by Gareth Bowler

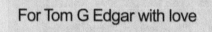

For Tom G Edgar with love

For commissions and queries email misspotterltd@gmail.com

Special thanks to

Michele Beadle, reader assistant at Hull History Centre, for verification of the historical
content in this book.

Published by F.J. Beerling © 2022

Josie the Jet was afraid to fly, and she was scared of heights,
Not ideal for a passenger plane, built for holiday flights.

"It's just no good," cried Josie,
As into the hangar she backed.
All she needed was reassurance;
It was confidence that she lacked.

Then dear Old Bob the bi-plane, who was teaching Josie to fly.

Just flew in from Manston Airport and saw the little jet cry.

So Bob, had an idea that was sure to make her feel better.

First he had to stop Josie crying, the floor was getting wetter.

As Josie cried, the cleaner arrived and began to mop the floor.

Her tears had made a little puddle, that reached the hangar door.

"Don't you worry," cried Bob, "well soon have you up in the sky.

You just need to believe in yourself, then you'll be flying high!

Josie felt much better now,
    She even ventured outside.
"I WILL fly those holiday makers,"
    The little jet replied.

    So she fired up her engines and taxied down the runway,
    Almost hitting the Turbo Twins, as they were heading their way.

    "Oh dear," cried Josie, panicking, as she turned herself around.
    The Twins teased and laughed at her, as she skidded along the ground.

So she headed for the hangar, and hurried back inside.
Then backed herself into a corner: Josie wanted to hide.

"Don't you worry," cried Bob,
"You'll propellers will get in a whirl!!
"But the Twins are right," sobbed little Josie,
"I am just a silly girl."

Old Bob smiled, then he cried: "I'm going to tell you a story,
About a lady, who against all odds, flew herself into glory!"

As Bob coaxed Josie back outside, and into the summer sun,

The cleaner had finished mopping the floor and was chewing on a bun!

And so Bob said to the little jet: "Amy Johnson was her name,

All she wanted to do was fly, but landed herself in fame."

"**H**ow did she do that?" quizzed Josie,

"By being a woman that's how!

Women travelled mostly as passengers; not pilots, like they do now."

Josie looked a bit puzzled, even the cleaner pulled a face!

Bob continued with his story; of Amy, the flying ace…

"…Amy was born in 1903,

When women stayed home and made the tea,

Washed the dishes, and raised the kids,

So dads could earn the money."

Amy went to school then University: working hard for her degree,

But she only ever wanted to fly; have adventures, be brave and free.

So she gained her pilot's license and also in the same year,

Amy became the first British woman to qualify as a ground engineer.

Not only could she fly a plane, she fixed them when they broke.

Fuelled them up and changed their oil, unheard of by womenfolk!

Amy desperately needed a plane but money was ever so tight.

So Daddy chipped in with a businessman;

Amy's dream was now in sight.

They paid for Jason the Gypsy Moth,

Wood and cloth, with two small wings.

It would fly Amy all over the world,

And could do loops, twists and spins!

Josie was feeling much happier now,

The turbo Twins had disappeared,

And Colin the cleaner was sipping his coffee,

He now had a frothy beard.

Bob shared more of Amy's adventures,

How she flew across the land,

With little ore than a map and compass

And no-one to hold her hand…

…No mobile phone or Sat - Nav, no canopy to keep her dry.

Just a coat and a pair of goggles

To stop the wind from making her cry!

Amy did an extraordinary thing, in 1930 on the 5th of May,

When she took off from Croydon Airport, scared but on her way.

Very few people waved her off, but the papers did give her a mention.

Then word got out as Amy flew all about and soon drew a lot of attention.

On her way to sunny Oz,

And her life wouldn't be the same.

After Amy flew 10 hours a day and thousands of miles in her plane.

*T*hrough the storms she battled and the shark infested sea,

Crashing her way to Darwin, Australia; Amy became a celebrity.

"*...B*ecause no other woman had done it,

And Amy had done it solo,

By flying from London to Australia, and the first woman pilot to do so.

"Amy was given cars and planes, the King gave her special praise,

During a 6-week tour of Australia, with 47 speeches in just 4 days!

Amy also broke flying records and flew during World War 2.

She was happy serving her King and country…

Then into the clouds she flew…"

Said Bob to Josie, as he looked around,

But Josie was up in the sky…

"If Amy can do it," shouted the little jet, "then why on earth can't I !"

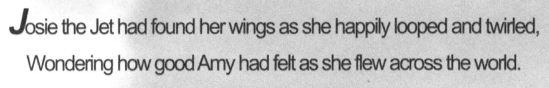

Josie the Jet had found her wings as she happily looped and twirled,

Wondering how good Amy had felt as she flew across the world.

Colin the cleaner clapped and cheered,

As Bob took him for a ride,

High above the fluffy clouds, a spare propeller strapped to the side.

Amy's story taught Josie a lesson;

Believe in yourself and never give up,

Don't worry what people think,

Be first, they'll soon catch up!

Amy's beloved plane, Jason is now on permanent display in the Flight Gallery at the Science Museum in London.

SPITFIRE GIRL

F.J. BEERLING

Spitfire Girl

By

F.J. Beerling

Published by F.J. Beerling

Her life in flight - the story of Jackie Moggridge for children of all ages…

…"You're nothing but a stupid girl!" jeered her two young brothers Eddie and Laurence. Jackie retorted "I'll show you!" And that's exactly what she did!

Captain Jackie just loved to fly! Adventurous, determined, full of fun and flying free she flew herself into the history books.

A WW2 pioneer in a man's world paving the way for women in aviation. Her love of flying propelled her through prejudice and adversity to realise her dreams.

Captain Jackie always believed that with hard work and determination "Anyone can achieve anything!"

In memory of Captain Jackie Moggridge – wife, mother, grandmother and Spitfire girl.

May all your goals and dreams come true.

Her daughters Veronica and Candy hope that her adventures in these beautiful snap shots of her life will inspire more girls to fly.

WW1 had ended - it was the 1920's and there was a boom in construction. Cars were being mass produced and electricity was being introduced into homes across Europe.

Mass production made technology affordable and as a result the film and radio industry also boomed…

…And aviation took off - literally!

Technology advanced rapidly, military and civilian aviation grew and record-setting, record-breaking flights captured headlines and public interest.

And in South Africa on March 1st in 1920, a baby girl was born. Her name was Dolores Theresa Sorour, and she would go on to become a pioneering pilot, an amazing aviatrix and a record-breaking woman of her time…

…And this is her story.

Can you spot her? Jackie is seated
third row down second from the right
Jackie at her convent school in Pretoria
South Africa.

"When we are very young, the grown-
ups talk as though we cannot hear.
'poor Jackie' mother says aloud, with
poor me standing near."

- Jackie Moggridge

Dolores hated her name so she decided to call herself Jackie, after her hockey-playing sports heroine Jackie Riddik.

Jackie (as she insisted on being called), lived with her parents and two brothers in Pretoria in South Africa.

There was always sibling rivalry between Jackie and her brothers. They would often tease her and one day, as a plane flew overhead, they called Jackie a sissy. Jackie looked up, pointed at the aeroplane and announced, "I'm going to be a pilot!"

So, to impress her teasing brothers, Jackie took an Aviation Correspondence Course from America. When the letter arrived, although it was addressed to 'Miss Jackie Sorour,' the certificate letter referred to Jackie as he and him...

...with an added letter 'S' written in pen changing he to a she!

Proudly, Jackie showed the letter to her brothers who weren't impressed, "You haven't even been up in an aeroplane!" they scoffed.

Jackie with her mother and two brothers in their garden.

AVIATION INSTITUTE of AMERICA, INC.

1115 Connecticut Avenue
WASHINGTON, D.C.

November 24, 1938
18044

Miss Jackie Sorour
136 Schoeman St.
Pretoria
Transvaal, S. Africa

TO WHOM IT MAY CONCERN:

This certifies that the bearer of this letter has satisfactorily completed a comprehensive course of study, preparatory for Aviation work and has attained high grades as a result of his efforts.

She has evidenced proof of an accurate understanding of airplane and engine construction, operation and maintenance--he understands the basic principles of Aeronautics and has creditably passed rigid examinations designed to test his understanding of the fundamental ground work necessary in Aviation.

I am confident that he will make a capable and diligent worker when given an opportunity to apply his training to practical work.

I respectfully recommend him for your consideration.

Very sincerely yours,
AVIATION INSTITUTE of AMERICA, INC.

Walter Hinton

WH:REC

President.

That soon changed when Jackie's mother paid for her to fly in a DH Rapide for her fifteenth birthday. Up she went and out it all came - poor Jackie was airsick!

But Jackie wanted glory over her brothers, so she asked her mother if she would pay for another flight for her next birthday.

Jackie went back up in a plane and this time she caught the flying bug; it would stay with her for the rest of her life.

ZS-ABH

Jackie's first solo flight!

It was in 1936, when Jackie was just 16, that she learnt to fly!

Not only did she gain her pilot's licence, she was also the youngest person in South Africa to do so.

This was the first of many achievements for Jackie.

When she was 17, she became the first woman in South Africa to do a parachute jump - in a parachute way too big for her - it was designed for a man to wear not a woman!

This didn't put her off, Jackie went up 5000 feet, clambered onto the wing and terrified she jumped. On landing, SNAP she broke her ankle…

…That was her first and last parachute jump!

Jackie with her mother Veronica

Jackie wanted to become a commercial pilot after meeting Doreen Hooper. Doreen Hooper was the first woman to gain a commercial pilot licence…

…So, to pay for her licence, Jackie flew sight-seeing tours before coming to England in 1938 to train as a commercial pilot in Witney, Oxford.

"Flying and my motorbike, injected me with confidence. We would roll along, friends, reluctant to turn back, anxious to explore together the next hill, the next horizon."

Jackie with her motorbike named Jill

"6000 miles south on a mountain side. The birth of my impossible dream nurtured my desire to fly."

- Jackie Moggridge

22nd June

LESSONS IN FLYING FROM P.O. "JACKIE"

Evening Citizen Reporter

EYE-CATCHING   visitor

Prestwick airport today w

a trim figure in Royal Air For

battledress, proudly wearing pilot

ings.   The flier — Pilot-Offic

WITNEY

TWINNED WITH
LE TOUQUET - FRANCE
UNTERHACHING - GERMANY

Jackie was one year into her course when WW2 broke out on October 2nd 1939.

Rejected by the Royal Air Force (RAF) who didn't allow women pilots then, Jackie joined the Women's Auxiliary Air Force (WAAF), hoping to work with planes - instead, she was made a cook!

Hopeless at cooking, Jackie was soon transferred to train on important and secret RADAR where she watched the Battle of Britain, by looking at a series of dots on a screen.

RADAR stands for Radio Detection and Ranging.

Pauline Gower who was also a keen pilot established the women's branch of the Air Transport Auxiliary (ATA), in December of 1939, and became its first commander.

The ATA ferried planes from factories to the frontline. The men ferrying the planes were themselves frontline pilots, now unfit for frontline service and were dubbed, 'Ancient and Tattered Airmen.' Their motto was, 'Anywhere to Anywhere.'

Pauline Gower was tasked with recruiting as many female pilots as possible to assist the male pilots with their workload. In 1940, Jackie was invited to Hatfield, where she became the fifteenth woman pilot in the ATA in number 15 ferry pool - an all-woman pool based at Hamble near Southampton.

Jackie was also the youngest female there!

Jackie is standing in the top row sixth from the left

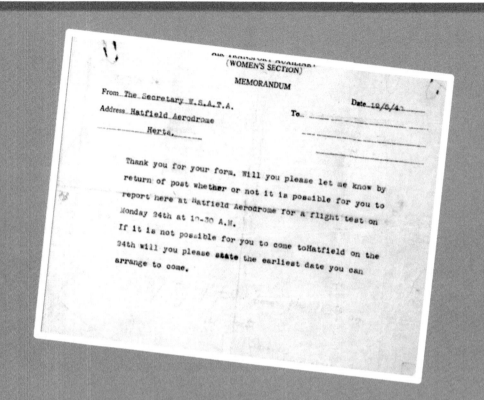

AIR TRANSPORT AUXILIARY
(WOMEN'S SECTION)

MEMORANDUM

From The Secretary W.S.A.T.A.

Address Hatfield Aerodrome

Herts.

Date 19/6/4

To

Thank you for your form. Will you please let me know by
return of post whether or not it is possible for you to
report here at Hatfield Aerodrome for a flight test on
Monday 24th at 10-30 A.M.
If it is not possible for you to come toHatfield on the
24th will you please state the earliest date you can
arrange to come.

For Jackie this was the opportunity she had been hoping for - flying again and doing her bit for King and country.

Another first for Jackie and all the other ATA girls…

…And a first for the male fighter pilots and engineers too - they weren't used to seeing women in the cockpits. "By Jove, you're a girl!" said one engineer when Jackie climbed out of the cockpit. "Yes," she replied brightly.

Jackie was flying high as a flying officer in uniform.

The ATA had 1,152 male pilots and 168 female pilots. Women no longer stayed home and made the tea - women ferried planes and drank the tea! Some even fixed the planes; they had trained to become ground engineers…

…And speaking of fixing, the ATA also ferried new planes that could be faulty and old planes that were mostly faulty. The old planes were destined for the scrapheap and ferrying them to their final destination was called, 'the graveyard flight.'

There were no radios so the pilots were unable to contact the ground crew. They were not allowed to fly into or above cloud level and they were not allowed to fly at night.

One of Jackie's first flights was to Scotland. On landing at the base of a fighter squadron she was approached by the camp's Commanding Officer. Seven of his fighter planes had gone down and none of the other pilots would fly. He ordered Jackie to get into an aircraft and take off - his plan worked, seeing a women fly, the other pilots also took to the skies!

Too dangerous for men? Then Jackie steps in …

No.15 Ferry Pool
Hamble

Jackie

They were given pocket-sized flip-pads - one-page per plane, instructions for all 147 types of plane; along with a map and compass.

The women were paid less than the men for doing the same job as the men. So, Pauline Gower campaigned for her girls to get equal pay.

Her efforts were rewarded in 1943, when her ATA girls received the same pay as the men...

...Although they were still not allowed to be promoted or enter the Officers Mess - that was for men only.

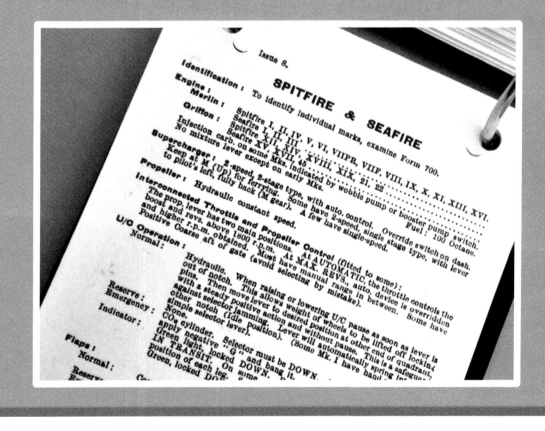

Issue 8.

SPITFIRE & SEAFIRE

Identification : To identify individual marks, examine Form 700.

Engine :
Merlin : Spitfire I, II, IV, V, VI, VIIPR, VIIF, VIII, IX, X, XI, XIII, XVI.
Seafire I, II, III.
Griffon : Spitfire XII, XIV, XVIII, XIX, 21, 22 ....
Seafire XV, XVII, 45 ....

Injection carb. on some Mks. indicated by wobble pump or booster pump switch. Override switch on dash. **Fuel :** 100 Octane. No mixture lever except on early Mks.

Supercharger : 2-speed, 2-stage type, with auto. control. Some have 2-speed, single stage type, with lever to pilot's left, fully back (M gear). A few have single-speed.
Keep at M (Up) for ferrying.

Propeller : Hydraulic constant speed.

Interconnected Throttle and Propeller Control (fitted to some) : At AUTOMATIC, the throttle controls the boost and revs. above 1800 r.p.m. At MAX. REVS., auto. device is overridden and higher r.p.m. obtained. Most have manual range in between. Some have Positive Coarse aft of gate (avoid selecting by mistake).
The prop. lever has two main positions.

U/C Operation :
Normal : Hydraulic. When raising or lowering U/C pause as soon as lever is out of notch. This allows weight of wheels to be lifted off locking pins. Then move lever to desired position at other end of quadrant, with a steady positive action and without pause. Lever will automatically spring against selector jamming. (Some Mk. I have hand ....
other notch (Idle position). This is a safeguard
simple selector lever).
Reserve : None. Selector must be DOWN.
Emergency : CO₂ cylinder, locked DOWN, and bang it.
Indicator : Green light.   apply negative "G," and bang it.
IN TRANSIT. On some ...
Green, locked DOWN. ...

Flaps :
Normal : position of each leg.
Reserve : Co...

Not only were there 147 different types of planes to fly, the ATA pilots also flew up to five different types in one day!

On the 13th of October in 1941, Jackie flew her first Spitfire from Crawley to Ternhill. By the end of the war, she had flown 83 different types of planes, and delivered 1,438 of the 309,011 that the ATA had delivered overall.

Jackie had flown 465 Spitfires during the war, and another 102 Spitfires after the war - a total of 567 Spitfires during her lifetime…

…And on the 29th of April in 1944, Jackie flew Spitfire ML407 to the New Zealand fighter pilot ready to fly on D Day.

"They were so sensitive and ladylike, made for a woman, it felt like you had wings."

Jackie so excited to fly her first Spitfire

It was whilst working in Radar at Rye that Jackie had met Captain Reg Moggridge from the Royal Engineers. They fell in love and were married on the 12th of January 1945.

Jackie's wedding dress was not only beautiful, but it had been beautifully made - by Jackie herself - using parachute silk because, like food, material was also rationed.

Finally, on the 8th of May 1945, the news that everyone had been hoping for arrived. The war was over!

The announcement was made by Prime Minister Winston Churchill. His speech was aired across the airwaves. Peace was declared and women were told to go home and become housewives again...

Not Jackie, Jackie wanted to carry on flying, so she joined the Women's Royal Air Force WRAF(VR). She flew for six years until the WRAF was disbanded.

To the left, Jackie and Reg on their engagement, and below on their wedding day…

…with Jackie's beautiful parachute silk wedding dress!

Just one year after the war had ended in 1946, Jackie was awarded the King's Commendation for Valuable Services in the Air.

By the KING'S Order the name of
First Officer Dolores Theresa Moggridge,
Ferry Pilot, No. 15 Ferry Pool, Air Transport Auxiliary,
was published in the London Gazette on
1 January, 1946,
as commended for valuable service in the air.
I am charged to record
His Majesty's high appreciation.

C. R. Attlee

Prime Minister and First Lord
of the Treasury

The awards kept on coming. In 1953, Jackie was awarded the Queen's Coronation Medal - this award was not on universal issue at the time, giving Jackie further recognition of merit. Then on the 26th of August in the same year, Jackie received her full RAF Wings.

The award ceremony took place at Wellesbourne, Mountford. After Jackie took her wings test in an Airspeed Oxford.

Jackie was the second of only five women to be awarded their full RAF Wings, before women were disallowed. The other four were, Jean Lennox-Bird (first), Benedetta Willis, Joan Hughes and Freydis Leaf.

Jackie   Freydis Joan Jean Benedetta

Billet

NAL HEALTH SERVICE No.   (10)   N

C.N.R.O.

(11) **COURSES OF**

COURSE PLACE AND DATE

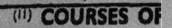

Awarded full R A F "wings" on 26/8/53

It was between 1954 and 1955, that a team of four (three men and one woman - Jackie) flew Spitfires to Burma. The trips were extremely dangerous as they flew mostly across the desert with the countries below at war.

They flew four Spitfires each trip, thirty Spitfires in total, stopping only nine times on route.

Every time they stopped; the aerodrome would search for the fourth pilot…

…Not believing that he was in fact, a woman!

It was another first for Jackie when she became the first British woman to unofficially break the sound barrier in a jet. However, no-one she asked would help her make it official.

Jackie continued to push the barriers - she still wanted to become a commercial pilot and finally in 1957 she succeeded.

She Asks Duke To Help Her 'Faster Than Sound' Attempt

By Sunday Dispatch Reporter

UNABLE to get Air Council or Air Ministry support for her plan to be the first woman to crash through the sound barrier, glamorous Mrs. Jackie Moggridge is asking the Duke of Edinburgh to help her.

Mrs. Moggridge, housewife, mother, and amateur ballet dancer, sat down at her home in Taunton, Somerset, last night and wrote him a letter.

It stated: "For some months now I have been applying to various authorities at the Air Ministry to assist me to fly a jet aircraft faster than sound, to claim the women's world record for Britain in this year of the Coronation.

"Although the authorities seem very enthusiastic about the attempt, no one will accept the responsibility and I, as a mere housewife, cannot hope to achieve so tremendous a project without help from her Majesty's Government.

Mrs. Jackie Moggridge.

3,000 Hours' Flying

"I have flown 3,000 hours solo, mainly on high-speed fighter and bomber aircraft, ferrying them

HIGH-FLYING PILOT TURNS AUTHOR

When Jackie wasn't busy flying…breaking the sound barrier…enjoying being a wife and mother, she was busy writing all about her experiences in the sky!

In 1957, Woman Pilot was published and many years later, in 2004, it was republished and given a new title, 'Spitfire Girl, my life in the sky,' by Jackie Moggridge.

Woman Pilot

'JACKIE' MOGGRIDGE

Now republished with photographs from Jackie's private collection.

Word got out and news of Jackie's exploits soon reached the Director of Channel Airways.

Jackie was summoned into his office, if she could pass the exam that nine of his male pilots had just failed, Jackie would be hired...

...Jackie did pass the exam and was hired...!

Jackie tried many jobs before flying for Channel Airways. One of which was flying fridges back to South Africa!

Working for Channel Airways, Jackie became the first British female Airline Captain to ferry passengers on scheduled flights.

To her boss and her colleagues Jackie was a pilot like any other. But her identity was kept secret, because if the passengers found out that their pilot was women it would make them nervous, so she was not allowed to broadcast announcements.

Juggling being a housewife and a full-time pilot meant that Jackie's young daughter Jill got to fly with Mummy from time to time - something that Jill's classmates could only dream of.

As well as Veronica Jill, Jackie has another daughter, Candida Helen and although they were born fifteen years apart they formed a close bond and, along with their father Reg, they fully supported their mother and her life in flight.

Jackie continued to fly and achieve great things. In 1958, she was awarded the Jean Lennox-Bird Trophy by the British Women's Pilots Association (BWPA) for, 'Outstanding Woman Pilot of the Year,' and for many more years, Jackie continued to fly commercially.

The largest plane that Jackie flew was a Viscount and in 1966, and again in 1969 and 1998, Jackie was invited to HM the Queen's garden parties for furthering the cause of women in aviation.

Jackie with her
Youngest daughter
Candida Helen
enjoying a ride to
the shops

Flying into Mummy's arms
Jackie pictured above with
her older daughter Veronica
Jill

In 1994, at age 74, Jackie flew her last Spitfire. She was re-united with Spitfire ML407 making this a total of 568 Spitfires that she had flown during her lifetime. Jackie passed away peacefully on the 7th of January 2004, aged 84.

Her lifetime was so different from many other women of her time. Working in a man's world, Jackie did not want to stay home and cook the tea. Jackie wanted to fly, be free, have adventures up in the sky where her spirit could soar…

…And her spirit lives on. Not only through her children and grandchildren, not only through the many books and news articles about her but also through the trophies that have been named after her. The WPA Jackie Moggridge Trophy inspires civilian women pilots, and the RAF Jackie Moggridge Trophy is awarded annually to the best "Female Aircrew or Engineer who has Demonstrated Outstanding Potential." - just like Jackie did.

Jackie flying ML407 again with Carolyn Grace 29/4/94 - exactly 50 years from the day she first flew it from the factory on 29/4/44.

Jackie's ashes were scattered by Carolyn Grace from Spitfire ML407, over Dunkswell Aerodrome near Taunton. There is a road in Taunton named after Jackie, it's called, 'Jackie Moggridge Way,' and two blocks of flats also named after her in Witney, they are called, 'Moggridge Walk.'

Flying High

My wings rise high

To join the race

Of scudding clouds across the blue

Exhilarating sky and pace

That's filled with heavenly peace and grace

Earth why should I return to you?

The sky is such a lovely blue

Oh Earth why should I return to you?

- Jackie Moggridge

I miss the beauty of that world,

Above the earth and I behold,

A vision there of silver wings,

And listen to my heart it sings,

It is not I that feels that thrill,

Though yet the memory lingers still,

It is a younger one today,

Whose flying now, o'er my skyway.

- Jackie Moggridge

Jackie Moggridge 1920 - 1984

Granny Jackie with her grandchildren Ash and Lara celebrating her 80th Birthday. Ash and Lara enjoyed many a flying adventure story with Granny Jackie.

Candy gives talks about her mother in schools, aeroclubs, societies and museums to keep her mother's legacy alive, inspiring girls to fly.
Contact details from, jackiemoggridgespitfiregirl.com

Printed in Great Britain
by Amazon

27802258R00044